The
Boston Tea Party

by Lori Mortensen
illustrated by Gershom Griffith

PICTURE WINDOW BOOKS
a capstone imprint

Special thanks to our advisers for their expertise:

Kevin Byrne, Ph.D., Professor of History
Gustavus Adolphus College, St. Peter, Minnesota

Terry Flaherty, Ph.D., Professor of English
Minnesota State University, Mankato

Editor: Jill Kalz
Designers: Abbey Fitzgerald and Tracy Davies
Art Director: Nathan Gassman
Production Specialist: Jane Klenk
The illustrations in this book were created with watercolor.

Photo Credits: cover (leather texture), Shutterstock/Leigh Prather; 2 (parchment texture),
Shutterstock/AGA

Picture Window Books
151 Good Counsel Drive
P.O. Box 669
Mankato, MN 56002-0669
877-845-8392
www.picturewindowbooks.com

Printed in the United States of America in North Mankato, Minnesota.
092009
005618CGS10

All books published by Picture Window Books
are manufactured with paper containing at least
10 percent post-consumer waste.

Library of Congress Cataloging-in-Publication Data
Mortensen, Lori, 1955–
The Boston Tea Party / by Lori Mortensen ; illustrated by Gershom Griffith.
p. cm. — (Our American story)
Includes index.
ISBN 978-1-4048-5538-0 (library binding)
1. Boston Tea Party, 1773—Juvenile literature. I. Griffith, Gershom, ill. II. Title.
E215.7.M67 2010
973.3'115—dc22
                                           2009029403

It was a cold December night. A group of men raced onto the ships. They carried axes. Thousands of people stood quietly and watched.

The ships in Boston Harbor were full of British tea.
But no one would be drinking it.

What happened that night in 1773 changed
history. It was called the Boston Tea Party.

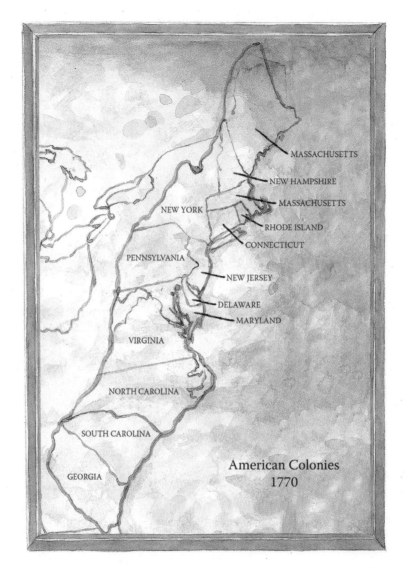

MASSACHUSETTS

NEW HAMPSHIRE

MASSACHUSETTS

NEW YORK

RHODE ISLAND

CONNECTICUT

PENNSYLVANIA

NEW JERSEY

DELAWARE

MARYLAND

VIRGINIA

NORTH CAROLINA

SOUTH CAROLINA

GEORGIA

American Colonies
1770

In the 1700s, America was made of 13 colonies. The Colonies belonged to Great Britain. They were ruled by King George III and the British government.

At first, the Colonists lived in peace. The British sent supplies and kept the Colonies safe.

KING GEORGE III

In 1754, Great Britain and France went to war. They fought for control of lands in North America, Europe, and Asia. They fought for control of the seas. The war lasted seven years.

In the end, Great Britain won. But it had very little money left. The British government decided to collect money from the Colonists.

The British put taxes on everyday things the Colonists used. They taxed sugar, glass, paper, and tea.

The Colonists got mad. Taxing them wasn't right. It wasn't fair!

When the Colonists protested, the king wouldn't listen. So they fought back. They stopped buying British goods.

The boycott angered the king. In 1768, he sent British troops to Boston. Soldiers filled the streets. They kept the Colonists under control.

But one snowy day in 1770, an argument broke out.
People shouted. A huge crowd gathered.

The soldiers fired, and five Colonists died.

News of what happened spread. Many Colonists wanted the soldiers to leave. To keep the peace, the king got rid of all the taxes—except one.

King George kept a small tax on tea. He did this
to show everyone that he was still in charge.

But the Colonists believed any tax was unfair.
Why wouldn't the king listen to them?

British tea? Forget it! Whenever ships brought tea into Boston Harbor, the Colonists wouldn't allow them to unload.

On December 16, 1773, three ships full of British tea sat in the harbor. They had been waiting there for weeks.

The sailors weren't allowed to unload their tea. And the ships weren't allowed to leave. They were stuck.

That night, thousands of people met in Boston. Samuel Adams and many other Colonists talked about fighting for their rights. It was time to act!

When the meeting was over, a group of men
disguised as Mohawk Indians raced onto the ships.

They chopped open 342 chests of British tea and dumped them into the water. The tea was ruined!

The king couldn't believe the news. The Colonists had to be punished! He sent more troops to Boston. Soldiers closed down the town and the harbor.

The Colonists worried. Which Colony would be next? For the first time, leaders from all 13 Colonies met. They would fight for freedom together.

27

The Revolutionary War began in 1775 and lasted eight years. In 1783, the Colonists won their freedom from Great Britain. The United States became a new country. And it all started one cold night at the Boston Tea Party.

Timeline

| 1754 | — | The French and Indian War begins between France and Great Britain. |

| 1764 | — | The government of King George III begins taxing the Colonists' everyday things. |

| 1770 | — | Five Colonists are killed by British soldiers in the Boston Massacre. |

| 1773 | — | The Boston Tea Party happens on December 16. |

| 1775 | — | The Revolutionary War begins. |

| 1776 | — | The Declaration of Independence is signed. |

| 1783 | — | The Revolutionary War ends. |

Glossary

argument—a talk between people who do not agree on something

boycott—the act of speaking out about something by refusing to buy certain products

Colonist—a person who lived in the 13 Colonies

colony/Colony—a land ruled by another country; one of the 13 British colonies that became the United States

disguised—dressed to look like someone else

harbor—a safe body of water near land for ships

Mohawk—a Native American tribe in New York

protest—to speak out against something

tax—a government fee

troops—soldiers

To Learn More

∽ More Books to Read ∽

—Espinosa, Rod. *The Boston Tea Party.* Edina, Minn.: Magic Wagon, 2008.

—Gunderson, J. *Ropes of the Revolution: The Tale of the Boston Tea Party.* Minneapolis: Stone Arch Books, 2008.

—Landau, Elaine. *Witness the Boston Tea Party with Elaine Landau.* Berkeley Heights, N.J.: Enslow, 2006.

∽ Internet Sites ∽

FactHound offers a safe, fun way to find Internet sites related to this book. All of the sites on FactHound have been researched by our staff.

Here's all you do:

Visit *www.facthound.com*

FactHound will fetch the best sites for you!

Look for all of the books in the Our American Story series:

—The Boston Tea Party

—The First American Flag

—The First Independence Day Celebration

—Paul Revere's Ride

—President George Washington

—Writing the U.S. Constitution